This book was given by

Aunt Lorraine & Uncle Carl

to

Gavyn James

as a remembrance of your Baptism

DECEMBER 16, 2007

For my parents, Erman and Betty,
who brought me to be baptized on August 30, 1964.

God Chose You

by Julie Dietrich
Illustrated by Kevin McCain

CONCORDIA PUBLISHING HOUSE · SAINT LOUIS

Long before you were even born,
God chose you as His child.
He called you as His little one,
Created you, then smiled.

God's loving plan then took a shape—
A baby, sweet and fine.
With little fingers and tiny toes,
In you, God's smile would shine.

People to love you, parents who care,
God surrounded you with love.
He placed special people in your life
While He watched you from above.

Which name would fit your little face—
A face so tender and fair?
God had chosen His very own name
For you to eternally bear.

God came to you. He welcomed you
On your Baptism day.
He made you part of His family.
"You are Mine," He seemed to say.

You were brought to the baptismal font.
Your parents and sponsors looked on.
The waters of Baptism touched your head.
The chains of sin were gone.

Baptized in the name of the Father,
And Jesus Christ, His Son.
Also in the Spirit's name,
The Trinity, Three-in-One.

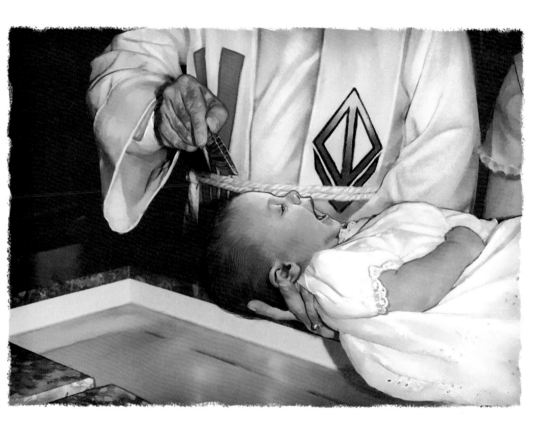

As bearer of God's holy name,
God calls you now to see
How lovingly He comes to you.
God's child you'll always be.

To keep you strong in your faith,
God's Spirit works in your heart.
God holds you in His loving arms.
From Him you'll never part.

The promise of heaven is now yours.
God's plan is now complete.
He's prepared a place for you.
In heaven, you'll one day meet.

Remember then your Baptism day,
Each day of every year.
God chose you as His little one,
A gift from God most dear.